I0558809

KAZUKO

Sixth Grade

in World War II

Hiroshima

KAZUKO

Sixth Grade
in World War II
Hiroshima

A MEMOIR

KAZUKO BLAKE

with

SANDRA VEGA

Copyright © 2024 by Kazuko Blake

All rights reserved.

Cover designer: David Vega

Published by

Wide Angle LLC
1111 S. Lincoln Ave. Unit 433
O'Fallon, IL 62269

LCCN: 2025417716

ISBN: 979-8-9908032-0-6 (hardcover)
ISBN: 979-8-9908032-1-3 (paperback)

Printed in the United States of America

Contents

for the memory of my parents

Foreword

Few people outside of my family have heard these stories, and even we seldom heard them. They are distinctive because of their close link to a famous moment in history. I call the dropping of the first atomic bomb over Hiroshima a famous moment in history because my generation learned about it in history class, but as the event moves farther into the past, it is fading from our culture's collective memory. August 6, 1945, seems so long ago. My mother is one of the few living survivors of that event, and this book relates her memory of it. It is a compilation of anecdotes from her life in Japan, a memoir of a childhood lived in a time and place of historical significance. This collection is meaningful to my mother, and therefore to me, and I have wanted to document it for many years. I am grateful she has agreed to share it.

Kazuko

Kazuko is an energetic, generous woman. Years ago, while visiting her (she was in her sixties or seventies), I turned the corner from the hallway to the family room and saw her sitting in a chair. It was such an unusual sight to see her sitting when it wasn't mealtime that I gasped, my heart skipped a beat, and I blurted out, "Are you ok?!" Her expression was quizzical, and when I indicated that I had never seen her "just sitting," her eyes grew big and round and she said, "What? I can't sit down?" She has a great sense of humor, too. She is now in her nineties, and her mind and that sense of humor are still sharp. She remembers the events recorded here like they happened yesterday.

She is always on the move, always doing something. She's a great cook and gardener, a highly accomplished seamstress and designer, and a Japanese-certified master of Ikebana, or flower arranging. All these things she does with unique flair, sharing with people who are fortunate enough to know her. She pokes fun at her early art lessons, but in truth, she has an excellent eye for design and has been a keystone in her jobs at textile and flower shops. After my siblings and I left home, she entered the workforce, part-time at first, then juggling as many as three part-time jobs and running her own business creating quilts and custom gifts. She worked mostly full-time until she was 80 years old, and like her father, she was a valuable employee whose bosses fought to keep employed with them.

It is also clear that she and her father had a close and special relationship. Her father, although steadfastly patriotic, had an unusually global worldview of things, understanding how differences between people and cultures could be bridged. He worked hard and was dedicated to his company, Mitsubishi, but he always made time for her. The bomb changed things for them, but I never heard a single complaint about that from my mother, other than displeasure with General MacArthur's suggestions to "improve" Japanese culture.

As we worked on putting her experience on paper, she mentioned several times that she was amazed at her mother's fortitude and energy. That spirit carried them through difficult days of war and postwar. I see that same spirit in her. I am amazed at her fortitude and energy. She created a beautiful home life in a new country with my father and built a sturdy foundation for my siblings and me.

In 2019, she returned to Japan for the first time to see my sister run in the Tokyo marathon. They visited the Peace Memorial Museum in Hiroshima, and seeing the efforts the city has made to ensure the past is not forgotten helped convince her to share her story. It is a unique and interesting story, partly because she is a unique and interesting person, but also because she lived in a time of great change in Japan.

Sandra Vega

Tajima Kazuko. Osaka, 1948.

Part I

Peace

Chapter 1

Background

How I got my name

I was born in Japan, in 1933, to Shigekazu and Aki Tajima. In those days, Japanese parents did not name their babies; that duty was passed to a trusted friend or family member. In my case, my father, Shigekazu (茂量), asked his best friend to name me. His friend made my name by using the last character of my father's name, "kazu" (量), and the character for "ko" (子), which is commonly used at the end of girls' names. Hence: Kazuko (量子). Unfortunately for me, the "kazu" in my father's name was written with a Japanese character (量) that is more commonly pronounced "ryu" or "ryo," so when people saw his name written, they would pronounce it incorrectly, as "Shigeryu." Since my father's friend named me using the unusual character of my father's name, my name caused me the same problems. No one ever saw my written name and called me Kazuko; they called me Ryoko. Kazuko is not an uncommon name in Japan, but the Japanese writing of my "Kazuko" is generally not known.

My father

My father's parents lived in Korea while my father was growing up. When it came time for my father to go to high school, he was sent to the only Japanese boarding school in Korea. He did well enough in high school to receive an opportunity to test for entrance into a top-tier university, and his heart was set on Todai (Tokyo Imperial University), the top college in Japan at that time. So, he took a ferry across the sea, intending to take a train to Tokyo to take the examination for entrance.

Unfortunately, he took the wrong train and missed the entrance exam. At that point, he had two options: wait a year to try again or wait a few days and test for entrance into his second-choice school,

Waseda University. He was deeply disappointed, I think heart-broken, but he didn't think waiting another year was an option for him. His father had paid for his travel to Tokyo and was planning to pay his tuition. There were no plans that included him waiting a year.

So, he waited the few days, tested at Waseda University, and was accepted. He enrolled, seemed to have had a busy and productive, if slightly wild, college experience, and then graduated from Waseda University a few years before I was born.

There was a worldwide economic depression happening then, so he was fortunate to get a job straight out of college working for a newspaper. He quickly learned that he didn't care for the newspaper business and switched jobs to the power company. He was fortunate to have that opportunity, too. The power company needed workers in Korea, and since he was familiar with the country, he was sent there, and my mother and I accompanied him.

After four or five years he applied for work at Mitsubishi, perhaps because he wanted to return to Japan. His boss at the power company and others advised him not to make that move, saying that as a

Waseda University graduate, he would not fit in well with the Todai University culture at Mitsubishi. His boss didn't want him to leave. His boss told him he would just be serving tea at Mitsubishi. But my father applied anyway, was hired, and we moved to Kobe.

Chapter 2

Kobe

A modern city with a beautiful beach

We lived in Kobe during my first, second, and third-grade years. We lived near a private beach, and when the weather was nice my father liked to swim in the ocean after work. He would take me along with him, and I would sit on the sand and watch him swim. My mother didn't think I should learn how to swim, because she worried that I would drown. My father responded that if I learned to swim, I wouldn't drown. They argued back and forth about it many times, but he couldn't convince her and eventually gave up trying.

I never learned to swim, but I did spend many hours sitting on the sand on that quiet beach watching him. I watched his form grow smaller and smaller as he swam out away from the shore, then larger and larger as he swam back. Sometimes he would swim out so far that I could barely see him, and I would call to him, but I never knew if he could hear me. Other times he would pause swimming, turn towards the shore and wave to me, then he would turn back to the open sea and continue swimming. Once he swam so long and so far from the shore I worried for him. He was so far away I couldn't see him clearly. I called for him, "Papa! Papa!" but he never bobbed up to wave. The sun began to set, waves continued to lap at the shore, and finally, he appeared as a tiny dot. It seemed to take forever, but his form slowly grew larger as he swam towards shore. When he finally did make it to shore, he said something about an invigorating swim. Nothing more.

Kobe was a modern city. While we were there, a new hair styling technique, the permanent, made its debut in some hair salons. Of course, my mother had to have one, and she was the first in our neighborhood to get one. She returned home transformed with a head full of curls, and when my father found out how much she paid for it, he asked, "Do you know how much I get paid?" Her answer: "Mmm. . .." That was the first time I wondered about money. I had accompanied her to markets after school sometimes, but she never asked about prices. Until then, I thought of money as just the means to get the things you want, and I hadn't thought about where it came from.

Before starting school, Papa's boss's wife brought gifts for me. She brought a pretty album which now contains photos of my youth and a pretty vase that she said I might put on my desk. School was important to Japanese people then, and starting it on a positive note helped set the tone for taking it seriously.

First Grade

At the beginning of the school year and on rainy or cold days, my mother met me after school and walked home with me. Sometimes we stopped for a snack on the way home: a hearty, filling bowl of noodle soup called udon. We often stopped at a shop where the owner, a kindly old man, made a special dish for me. He would bring a bowl of steaming hot udon out to me and declare that he had made it especially for me. But then at dinnertime, I wasn't hungry, and my mother fretted that I would become unhealthy because

I had such a poor appetite. She knew a lot about vitamins and nutrition but maybe not so much about the stomach capacity of a young schoolgirl!

My least favorite activity in first grade, and probably throughout the rest of my school days, was art class. People who know me now are often surprised to learn that because I design and make a lot of things using textiles. But drawing and painting are different, and they weren't fun for me. In class, whenever given the opportunity to draw or paint anything we liked, I drew the Japanese flag. After doing that many times, the teacher said we were to try to draw something new, something we hadn't attempted before. I think he might have been addressing me. So, I drew the Japanese Navy flag, which isn't much more complex. I repeated that a couple of times, then he requested something new, again! *Oh, no!* I thought and drew a simple boat to represent a Japanese navy ship, with the Japanese flag, of course! Then, that clever teacher brought a tomato, a banana, and an eggplant to school. He set them together on his desk, making a nice still arrangement for us to draw. Even today I remember the arrangement and the colors of the fruits. It was nice looking, fresh and inviting; but my artwork looked nothing like that pretty display! I used red, yellow, and purple crayons, but the finished work didn't look like anything at all; it was just colorful smudges.

My mother's response was something like, "What is that?" and she told my father, "You can only tell what it is by the colors. We have to do something about this."

The solution turned out to be my father doing many drawings with, or even for, me. My father was friends with my teacher, so maybe that's why the teacher ignored the situation. I find it amusing that now my son has a degree in art, but you can be sure I didn't help him with any of his assignments!

I liked reading class better than art class. One of my first homework assignments was reading. I had a small desk at home that was for doing homework. Most Japanese homes didn't have Western furniture, but we had some. I kept my pretty bud vase on the corner of my desk, and each day, while I was at school, my mother filled it with a single freshly clipped flower. It was nice to sit at my special place at homework time. I sat at my desk to do my reading assignment. A nearby window was open, and I could hear people outside. I practiced reading in the loudest voice I could. "Sakura, sakura, sakuraga, saita, koi koi! Inu koi!" "Koi! Koi! Inu koi!" I read aloud over, and over, so loudly, hoping the neighbors would hear me and know I was studying. I could be bashful sometimes at that age, but not in that moment!

Most other classes in school were fine for me, but what I really wanted to learn was how to play the piano. Unfortunately, there were no pianos available. War had not yet started, but companies had already stopped making them and were switching to making combat equipment. My mother searched everywhere but couldn't find a piano, so I gave up hope of learning to play. I would get a chance to learn a few years later, after the war ended, but until then I just focused on schoolwork.

Spending time with Papa

In Japan, the work week was six days long. Sundays were meant for relaxing, but every Sunday my father tried to spend time with me. He even tried to find time after work during the week to spend time with me. Many times, after school hours, he took me to the school playground and tried to teach me to pull myself over a bar that was like a low pull-up bar. I wasn't strong enough, but he tried and tried to teach me. He showed me how to hold the bar, but I never mastered it. For a long time, we went every day.

When I was a little older, he took me to another apparatus at the same playground, a swinging pole that hung from a much higher bar. I surprised him by climbing it easily, and he happily told my mother about it when we got home. She said, "She doesn't have to do that," because she didn't think girls needed to do such things, but I felt happy that he was proud of me.

Wartime pen pal

War started during the last term of my second-grade year. The school year was divided into three terms and started in April. There was a summer break in July and August, and there was homework to accomplish during that break. The second term ran from September through the middle of December. Winter break was mid-December to January 7, and included only light homework. The third term, January through mid-March, were the winter classes, or end-of-year classes.

During the winter classes of my second-grade year, schoolchildren wrote letters and sent care packages to combat soldiers. My letter went to a high-ranking army officer, a commander, I think. He wrote back to me, and we pen-palled for quite a while, even after my family moved to Hiroshima. But as the war started to go badly for Japan, I didn't hear from him. Shortly after the war ended, he wrote to my father to see how we were doing. He had safely returned to his home in Tokyo. I wrote to him, and we resumed our correspondence for a while, but eventually, we lost touch.

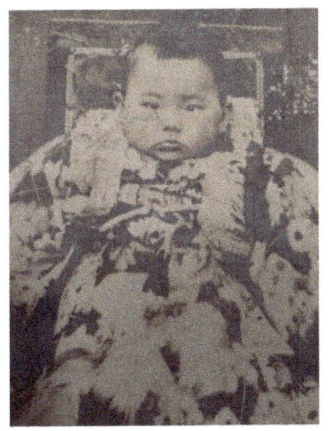

Tokyo, 1933

Shichi Go San event.
Special day for 3-, 5-,
and 7-year-old children.
I was 3-years old.
Nov 1936, Korea.

Outside our house in
Korea. We had huge
cherry trees in our yard.

In our backyard in Korea.

My mother often dressed me in white dresses. Korea, outside my father's workplace at the power company.

First day of 1st grade with my father. Apr 1, 1940, Kobe.

Mitsubishi's annual mushroom foraging. Papa had just recovered from a near-fatal case of influenza. Oct 5, 1941, Kobe.

First day of 2nd grade with my father.
Apr 1941, Kobe.

First grade class photo. The two adults are the school principal on the left and our class teacher on the right. First grade teachers move with their classes to second grade to make the grade transition smooth; he taught us for two years. The girl standing at the far right in the second from the top row is Kayoko, a talented pianist. Kobe, May 1940.

Singing and dancing in second grade. The school in Kobe was a good school with a concrete building. The student standing in front is our talented singer-conductor. Kayoko is standing alone in the front because she was playing the piano. Nov 1941, Kobe.

Part II
War

Chapter 3

Hello Hiroshima

Moving to Hiroshima

When Mitsubishi decided to open a shipyard in Hiroshima, my father and one engineer were sent from Kobe to help open and then expand it. It grew to be the largest shipyard in Asia. The move was an important one for my father's career. We were set up with housing near my school, south of the city center. There weren't many housing options near the school my father wanted me to attend, so when he found an available home, he requested it, and Mitsubishi approved it.

Looking back, I realize he always tried to find housing convenient to my schools, even if it meant a longer commute for him. He rode his bicycle to work, and I heard many of his coworkers exclaim that only a young person could bike that commute. I thought he was old, but other old people often exclaimed, "You're so young!" to him. So, then I wondered how old they were! At that time, my father was 42 and was the youngest person to hold his position in Mitsubishi's history. Now I understand why he seemed young to them.

After living in bustling Kobe, the school in Hiroshima seemed like a country school to me. Before leaving Kobe, my mother bought many school supplies and items she thought we might not be able to find in Hiroshima. When school started, we found that the girls in Hiroshima wore pants, unlike the girls in Kobe who wore skirts at that time. Almost immediately, Mother found a dressmaker who made a whole new wardrobe for me.

I loved watching the dressmaker cut fabric and fit them to me. I loved it so much my parents eventually bought a sewing machine for me. Sewing machines were already hard to find because of the war, but my father found a Mitsubishi brand machine for me. I learned everything I could about sewing from our seamstress and learned to take good care of my machine in the short time I had it.

The pretty pansies

After I learned the route to and from school, I walked it alone. I remember one part of the walk vividly. Along the way, there was a large Western-style house with pretty flowers in the front. I liked to stop and look at the flowers. Some were flowers that I hadn't seen before. Although the house was of Western style, the lady who lived in it was Japanese. She was friendly and spoke with me about the flowers. She said the flowers that looked like happy faces to me were called pansies, and they were common in America, where she had once lived. I was fascinated by those purple and yellow flowers and liked to just stand and look at them; they seemed to be smiling. Sometimes she invited me into the yard beyond the big iron gate and high stone wall. Sometimes she was indoors, and I didn't see her. Sometimes she was outdoors, and we bowed in greeting.

In Japan, people bow as a greeting, and the junior person does not rise from the bow until the senior person rises. I didn't have the patience for that, though, and I gave cursory bows sometimes. I must have done that with the lady who grew the pansies, because one day when I returned home from school my mother was outside the house waiting for me. She scolded me for rising from my bow too quickly. I was taken aback and couldn't figure out how she could have seen me. The sight line from my house to the Western-style house was blocked by other houses. It was confusing to me.

I don't have many memories of being scolded, but that is one I remember clearly. First, I couldn't figure out how she could have seen my bow, and then, in addition to that, she said I should bow and then count to ten before rising! Huh! After that, I found I sure could count to ten fast!

After moving to Hiroshima, my father's work responsibilities increased rapidly, and he kept longer hours at the office. On most weekdays he returned from work, quickly changed clothes, had a bite to eat, and headed back out to evening office functions. Usually, several of his coworkers came to our house in a limousine while he biked home, and they waited in our living room while he changed clothes. My mother served light dinner and tea, and I nabbed Father for quick homework help while the other men ate.

Bicycling with father

Despite his busy schedule, my father continued to try to spend time with me. In 4th grade, if the weather was nice, we often went on a bike ride. He had a carrier on the back of his bike, and I sat there while he pedaled. He would tell me to hold on tight and to not move. We rode through residential streets and past public places. People smiled and waved, and I had a grand time. He pointed out the various neighborhoods as we biked through residential areas unfamiliar to me.

Sometimes we biked by a corner manned by policemen. At first, the policemen nodded and smiled, but while we were stopped at an intersection, a policeman said in a friendly manner, "You know, Mr. Tajima, it is against the law to carry your daughter on the back of the bike like that." My father apologized politely, and we went on our way. But we didn't stop riding together and we didn't even stop going by the policemen's corner. The next time we encountered the policeman, he gave my father a ticket. Father accepted it apologizing politely, then the next morning he took the ticket to his friend, the head policeman at the Hiroshima police headquarters.

He tossed the ticket onto his friend's desk saying, "Do something about this."

The captain said, "Why do you ride in front of the police who stand there every day? You could ride a different route."

They had a good laugh together, but my father and I did stop riding by the poor dutiful policemen. We eventually stopped the bike rides entirely; I think I had grown too big to fit comfortably on his carrier! And maybe he thought we had pushed luck far enough.

Our neighbors in Hiroshima

Our home in Hiroshima was in a newly built neighborhood of duplexes. There were two duplexes lined up along the road, with another home sitting perpendicular to the duplexes at the end of the row. An army officer lived in the perpendicular house at the end. There was a large grassy space behind the houses that served as a nice backyard for everyone. From the street, looking toward the houses, ours was on the far left, at the end farthest from the army officer's home. Ours was the last house built and was the last home to be occupied.

The owner was pleased that we were the occupants. His daughter and son-in-law lived in the building next to ours. His son-in-law was nice to me and helpful, too. He taught me so much about my sewing machine that I eventually impressed even my father with my ability to make repairs on it. I soaked up knowledge of pattern making, piecing, and sewing from my dressmaker, but this man generously taught me how to use and care for the machine, skills I still use today.

A Mitsubishi contractor and his family lived next door to us, in the other half of our duplex, and his wife and my mother became good friends. They spent a lot of time together, and at some point, they decided it was bothersome for one of them to have to leave their house to get together to socialize or to check on one another to make sure everything was ok. Perhaps that happened after the neighbors had a baby in the summer of 1945, or maybe it was before, while she was expecting the baby. Whenever it was, their solution, my mother's idea, was to cut a small square hole in the wall between our houses! They left a paper flap that could be opened to reveal the hole (ever so convenient for checking on your neighbor or socializing through) or closed for privacy when the husbands were home.

They did the job neatly, but oh my goodness, my father was not happy about that! He carried on and on about it for days, because Mitsubishi had provided the house for us, and because it was a nice one. And of course, he thought it was a very silly thing to do. But when my mother got an idea in her head, there was no stopping her. She insisted it could be helpful in an emergency, and in this case, she would later be proven correct. I don't know how the neighbor's husband reacted to the hole in the wall, but I can't imagine he was too pleased, either. In the end, the owner never found out about it.

Chapter 4

War Intensifies

Clothing rules for citizens

After we moved to Hiroshima, the government ordered all schoolchildren to wear dark clothing. Japanese pilots reported that it was easier to spot movement on the ground if people were wearing light-colored clothing, so we all wore dark clothing, even in the summertime. The dark fabric was hot, so to keep cool, I wore a thin white cotton camisole, which we called a half-slip, under it. We also had to wear patches on our school clothes with our name, address, and blood type. In the wintertime, we were directed to wear a cotton-padded hood to protect our heads. We believed the enemy dropped bombs in more crowded places, so we tried to make it difficult for them to see us.

Building the bomb shelter

The government said each family should have a bomb shelter. They said it would be sufficient to build one inside a closet within the house, but my father said that a closet wouldn't do, and he had workers from Mitsubishi come to our home and build a bomb shelter in our backyard. Ours was L-shaped and the entrance was accessed two or three steps down into the ground. I never understood why it was built in an L-shape instead of a safer U-shape, but it was large enough to accommodate five people, and it served us well.

There were two heavy doors, slanted into the ground like an American Midwest storm cellar, painted with fireproof paint that I thought was an ugly color. Metal sheets covered the fireproofed doors and were painted green, a much better color I thought, to match the surrounding grass. The frame of the shelter was wood, and the interior was lined with shelves. The entire structure was covered with dirt and sod brought in from Mitsubishi grounds. Once the sod was laid, my father said, "now we can put flowers all the way around it," but my mother didn't like that idea. Instead, she filled our blue hibachi with soybeans and buried it in the ground three or four steps from the shelter's entrance. We didn't eat soybeans at home, but she evidently thought we should have them, perhaps because they store well. Father teased her about them, saying, "You just need a drop of water and you're going to get a lot of beansprouts!"

Mother filled the shelves with dried food, tin cans of tea, and rock crystal sugar. I knew about the sugar; I used to snitch some of it. Mother knew that if she didn't see me in the house, she would have to come and get me and restock the sugar crystals. Father commissioned a metalworker to build two metal boxes with lids to store clothing in the shelter. There was also a colorful hibachi crafted with gold and enamel paint which was special to my father. Mother filled it with water and changed it every day. While changing the water, she would say, "We'll use this someday, this will be a lifesaver someday." She did this every day, religiously, and I can still hear her voice chanting the words, sometimes to herself, as she worked.

Father joked about the hibachi filled with soybeans, but he never made fun of her daily efforts to refresh the water in the other hibachi. I still have that hibachi and the metal cans. I use the cans to store off-season clothing; they still bear the initials of the metalworker who built them for my father. We also had outdoor chairs in the backyard. If we were outside and sirens came, everybody moved from the chairs to the bomb shelter.

Bomb shelter practice run

Most houses were made of wood. The outer walls were plaster, and inside walls were made of paper screens. The whole structure was built on a platform made of wood. If the ground was uneven, there could be a small space, or even a crawl space, under part of the house. Our house had a small space under the hallway area. In traditional Japanese houses, a hallway runs along an outer wall, not through the middle of the house. The outside wall of the hallway is lined with windows, which lets sunlight into the hallway. The other side of the hallway is lined with sliding paper screens that serve as walls to the other rooms of the house. All the rooms in the house are along this inside wall of the hallway, and the paper screens can be arranged to let sunlight from the hallway into any room.

One day I was indoors while my mother was outdoors, at the front of our house, possibly cleaning the front door. It was a nice day. Suddenly an enemy airplane dove low toward her. Frightened, she hollered with a shockingly loud voice to take cover and go to the bomb shelter. I was startled by the sound of her voice—she was so loud I knew she wanted me out of the house.

I ran outside but I didn't think I had time to get to the bomb shelter. As she continued to holler frantically, I dove into the small space under the hallway and tried to crawl under the house. My back end was sticking out, and I was too scared to run across the yard to the bomb shelter, so I scraped harder at the dirt, trying to crawl under the house. The plane was roaring towards us, my mother was hollering in panic, and I was hoping the pilot would not hear her and see my back end sticking out and shoot me!

As the airplane passed, Mother ran towards me and shouted, "What are you doing there? Why didn't you go to the bomb shelter?!" And she laughed! Then the plane was gone, and we broke into an uncontrolled sidesplitting laughter about my desperate attempt to burrow under our house with my back end sticking out.

Father argues with military police

One day while in my backyard, I saw an airplane falling from the sky, going round and round as it fell, black smoke and flames trailing up into the sky.

Later that day I learned from my father that it had been shot down by our forces. It was a terrible day for my father, and he told my mother and I about it.

A fisherman found the enemy pilot's body floating in the ocean, and he brought it to shore leaving it on Mitsubishi property. He informed someone at Mitsubishi, but that person didn't know what to do with the body, so the problem was elevated until it landed with my father.

My father called the military police (MP) station and told them so they could take the proper measures, but the MPs told him that because the body was on Mitsubishi property, Mitsubishi had to prepare the body for burial and take it to the funeral home. My father was irate, saying that Mitsubishi hadn't shot him and therefore wasn't responsible. He argued so much that his coworkers feared he would get into trouble with the military or government. In the end, my father lost the argument, and Mitsubishi was forced to complete the duty. My father apologized to whichever worker was assigned the task and came home still angry about the incident. It seemed wrong and unfair, but it was a sign that our lives would not always make sense and that the confusion of war was creeping close to home.

Chapter 5

Wartime Protocols and Emergency Plans

Prohibitions and rationing

During those days, when the war was getting to be bad, no one could carry cameras. There was widespread fear that spies would take pictures of industrial places. For that reason, I don't have many photos of that time. Also because of the fear of spies, we weren't supposed to speak English in public places. That was very difficult for me because I had always called my father "papa" instead of the usual Japanese "otosan." "Papa—" would slip out before I realized I was speaking. I was nine years old when the language restriction first went into effect, and I found it very difficult to change. English signs in public places, even train stations, also disappeared.

The Europeans who ran businesses in the city had left early in the war, while we were still in Kobe, so the German and French bakeries were gone. There were no more stops at the French bakery for pretty sweets for me, and no more German bread to enjoy with coffee for my father. Common household items began to be rationed. The government collected jewelry for the war effort, and rubber was reserved for military use. I overheard my parents whispering about how bad things must be for the government to ask for people's jewelry. They wondered if the government would eventually ask for money from people's bank accounts.

My mother worried I would outgrow my shoes, so she bought tennis shoes in all sizes. That seems funny to me now because I didn't use tennis shoes. She also bought piles of notebooks and school supplies; and of course, there were all those soybeans! She stockpiled charcoal, rubber goods, special coffee for my father, sugar, and chocolate bars, specifically Hershey bars because they were my favorite. Eventually, coffee could only be found on the black market, then it too disappeared. My father switched to drinking black tea. I remember the tin was green with gold markings and the tea was from Ceylon. When that too disappeared, he switched to gyokuro, a type of Japanese green tea.

Looking back, I think my mother was an amazing woman for gathering so many supplies during that time. She was resourceful and proactive and tried anything she could think of to find food and supplies. So many women cried because it was so hard to get basic supplies, but somehow my mother persevered and found ways to get things she thought we needed.

Evacuation arrangements

As the war became more menacing, the city government in Hiroshima ordered families to make emergency evacuation arrangements. They suggested that nonessential families and children evacuate to the countryside or to relatives away from the city. Some adults who were part of the war effort sent their children to live with relatives in the country. We didn't know anyone in the Hiroshima area, so I stayed in town with my parents. My sixth-grade class in August 1945, had shrunk to about a quarter to a third of its first-term size since most students had evacuated with their families over the summer. Instead of five or six classes of sixth graders, there was only one, and it was small. Those of us who remained were supposed to have emergency evacuation plans.

We didn't have family nearby to help with that, but one man who worked for my father approached him saying, "Mr. Tajima, you can come to stay in my barn. You can fix it up a bit. Your family can stay there; there's nothing in the barn. You can cook anything you like and use the well."

The man was a part-time farmer who lived outside the city in a country house. He had a small orchard and a barn across the street from his house. Since he was also a Mitsubishi employee, he had not been drafted like other farmers. My father didn't have a backup location for us yet, but he didn't agree right away.

The man brought it up again, later, saying, "You can come to just look at it."

My father did go to see it. He thought it could work for us, so he had a top floor installed and finished with two rooms. Mitsubishi sent carpenters with truckloads of building materials to work on the barn. They built a nice staircase and installed a large picture window in one of the top-floor walls. It had a lovely view of the countryside stretching out to the beach. They also furnished the rooms with beds and some furniture. Downstairs, they fashioned a simple kitchen area on the bare dirt floor of the barn. It was designed around an existing well that had been fitted with a hand pump, and they set up a shichirin, an indoor grill for cooking.

We sent some clothes and pots and pans from our house to store there, in case we needed to evacuate. It was all completed before we ever needed it. My parents also sent a few cherished items there for safekeeping. My mother saved a mirror that was special to her, and an album of photos of me.

I believe my mother worried for my safety, although she never said so to me. Whenever I left the house, she wrapped a white cotton cloth around my waist like a money belt, under my clothes. She had sewn fifteen or twenty 10-yen bills into the folds of the cloth, making three or four separate sections for sets of five bills. The bills went all the way around my waist.

A 10-yen bill in 1945 was like a $1 bill and had the purchasing power of about $10 today. Each time Mother wrapped the cloth around my waist, she would tell me the money was "just in case. . . I don't think you need this, but just in case. . .," and she told me to use the bills one at a time, and to not let anyone see me take money out of the cloth. If I needed to access the money, she said I could go to a bathroom or private place to extract one bill, and I was to hold the bill discreetly, not flash it about. Each of the many times I left the house, she never failed to remind me. It was hot to wear in the summertime, and it was the first thing I happily discarded after the war ended.

School wartime drills

I learned to recognize airplanes by the sound of their engines. We were familiar with the sound of Japanese plane engines because we lived in Hiroshima, where friendly planes frequently flew. My house was near a large lumberyard that was situated on a river, and across the river was an airport. I liked to walk to the berm along the perimeter of the lumberyard to watch the airplanes. Hearing those planes overhead had never been cause for concern. They were part of our environment much like living near any airport is today. But the first time I heard an American plane overhead was startling; its sound was deeper, different. Usually, those planes flew too high to be heard, but when they flew low, I knew they were not our friendly planes. Later, after the war, a Japanese zero pilot described flying beneath a B-29 as feeling like a soybean on a tray, because the B-29s were so much larger.

As the tempo of war increased, the mood at school changed. We had emergency drills and elementary combat lessons. We practiced hiding under our desks and were taught how to protect ourselves in case our city was bombed. We were supposed to squat under the desk with backs rounded to protect our belly area and were to place our hands over our faces with our fingers and thumbs positioned to protect our eyes, nose, and ears. "Thumbs in ears, three fingers over eyes, pinkies hold nose, you can breathe through mouth."

We also had self-defense lessons. Poles were placed in the ground and were fashioned into makeshift human dummies, like crude scarecrows without heads. We practiced running at the makeshift enemies with poles, broomsticks, tools, anything really; we were told to use whatever was available. Some of the boys were especially enthusiastic about those drills, yelping and running hard at the practice poles. But truly we all wanted to do well, believing that we were training to help our military forces defend our mother country. We were quite serious about doing our part in the war effort.

We also learned farming techniques. We cleared a patch on the playground and planted vegetables. One day my father visited the school while we were planting. He had a friendly relationship with the school principal and visited sometimes, so I wasn't surprised to see him. But then I overheard him say to the principal, "Do you think this is necessary for children of this age?"

I was so embarrassed! And shocked. He had taught me about Japan's greatness, personal honor, love of country; I couldn't believe my ears! I cannot think of any other time in my life when I was not proud that he was my father. I thought we were learning good things, things that might help our country. People talked about fighting to the last man, and I took that literally. And if planting a garden was helpful to Japan, I wanted to learn about that, too.

Appendectomy

At the end of fifth grade, in March, I had my appendix removed. My father knew the war was turning bad, so he said I should have the operation then, even though it wasn't an urgent case. After my surgery, my father's boss's wife, Mrs. Niwa, brought a pretty brooch as a good luck gift. She gave the brooch to my nurse to give to me, because she was afraid that I might be too nervous to have a visitor. She was always nice to me. I remember having pretty bakery treats at her home when she invited my father and me to visit. I still remember her as being nice to me and giving pretty gifts.

During the evening after my surgery, while I was resting in my hospital bed with my mother sitting comfortably nearby, there was a huge bang! I asked my mother what it was. She didn't want to alarm me, so she said a nurse had bumped into something in the hallway. I couldn't imagine what the nurse could have bumped into to make that much noise, but things seemed calm enough afterward that I didn't worry about it. Mother stayed through the night with me, then went home in the morning.

Shortly after she left, my nurse came into my room and exclaimed, "Did you hear that bomb last night?" She seemed quite excited about it. I was about to ask about her noisy bump in the hallway, but she continued chattering on about the unexploded bomb that landed on the building next door. I realized that the loud bang had been a dud bomb, not my nurse in the hallway!

When my mother returned later that day and I tried to tell her about the bomb, she said maybe there was another bang that was the nurse. When I explained that it was my nurse who had told me about the bomb, she said maybe there was a different nurse who caused the bang that we heard. She really didn't want to admit there had been a bomb!

Before leaving the hospital, my whole class came to visit me and wish me well. That was nice and I appreciated seeing them very much. I completed the schoolwork for the spring term at home, on bed rest.

Surgical protocol during those days called for three months of bedrest plus three months of restricted activity after an appendectomy. I had the summer to continue recuperation. Since classes were often disrupted by drills and other wartime emergencies, summer breaks were usually short during the war. We had classes through at least part of each summer. In a way, that didn't bother me, because it meant I didn't have to keep a summer diary, which I disliked doing. I especially disliked having to make a daily weather report. When school resumed early in August 1945, I was well enough to study, though not yet medically cleared to take part in physical activities.

Chapter 6

August 6, 1945

Clearing the city center

During those days, families were required to help clear the city center of flammable timber to help control fires if we were bombed. Other cities had been firebombed, and Hiroshima residents wondered why Hiroshima hadn't been hit yet. Residents were afraid of becoming a target because Mitsubishi's largest plant was there. Bombs in other cities were dropped in crowded locations near flammable buildings. The central area of Hiroshima had many wooden structures. The city's government wanted to tear down houses in strategic locations to help control the spread of fire. They ordered each neighborhood to send two people every day for the work. The two people had to be from different families, and all families were to take turns. People from other cities helped, too. Sometimes people traded days or found substitutes to take their place in the work; that was allowed.

On August 6, our family and an army officer's family were each supposed to send one worker to represent our neighborhood. Normally the man of the house would go, but in both of our families, the men were needed at work for wartime reasons, so the duty fell to the wives. My mother was unable to do manual labor because heavy labor caused her face to turn red and puffy, and she had neck and shoulder problems.

My father found a replacement from work, an older man who lived near the tear-down area. My father thought he was doing the man a favor by sending him as a substitute, because he would not have to go to work that day, and he would have a shorter day. The man was grateful and expressed many thanks. My father told him that once he had finished in the city center, he could go home and enjoy the rest of the day off. Father thought he was being nice to the man.

The army officer's wife had two children: a three-year-old girl and a three- or four-month-old baby. My mother agreed to watch the children while the woman did the city work. But then other people convinced our neighbor to take her small baby with her, because burdened with a baby, she probably would not be asked to do heavy work. They told her that she would most likely be asked to serve tea to the workers and might even be released early. They had seen that happen with other young mothers. She took their advice, and my mother watched the three-year-old girl while our neighbor, carrying her baby, went to help in the city-clearing effort.

Every day those assigned to do the city work gathered outdoors and traveled together to the city center. That morning my father waited at home for the worker who was going to replace him. Their agreed-upon meeting time, 7:00, passed.

Another minute or so passed, then my father said, "I wonder what happened to him."

My mother said, "Maybe he is sick, or something."

Then my father declared, "I'm going to go with them," referring to the people assigned to timber-clearing duty.

He sat down to put on his shoes to join the neighbors going to the city center. He was dressed for work in a suit and tie, because he wasn't expecting to miss work, but he certainly wouldn't send my mother to do the laborious work in the city.

He was tying his shoes and saying, "If he shows up, send him our way. I'll trade—" when the man showed up.

I saw the older man bowing repeatedly and apologizing profusely for being late, maybe three minutes late.

My father said, "Oh, we were just talking about if you were to come."

They exchanged best wishes for the day, then the man went on his way with the army officer's wife and others from nearby neighborhoods, and my father went to work as originally planned. Sadly, we never saw that man again.

I had been getting ready for school while listening to and watching the adults. That day I wore a long-sleeved black blouse made from one of my mother's black summer kimono. The fabric was beautiful silk, and there were small red buttons down the front. I wore a white half-slip (camisole) under the blouse. After my father and his clearing duty substitute left the house, sirens began blaring. My mother and I and the three-year-old girl went to the bomb shelter. Nothing happened, so my mother went back into the house with the toddler, and I went to school.

August 6, 1945, 8:00 am

It was a very bright, very sunny morning. Later we were told the enemy had wanted a clear day. Our shortened summer break was over, and we were just a few days into the second term. I was recovering from the appendectomy and was not supposed to take part in morning exercises or vigorous activity. Every morning all students and teachers met outside on the playground near the school building to exercise before class instruction began. We exercised for 20-30 minutes to radio music, the principal gave a short speech, then we filed into the building for classes. I didn't want anyone to think I was being lazy, so for the first days after the summer break, I hadn't refrained from morning exercises. Somehow my parents found out.

"Kazuko, you know you are not supposed to do exercises."

"I know, but I'm not *really* doing them. I just move my arms, like this," I said, waving my arms half-heartedly.

My parents had known what I was doing. They knew that I didn't want to stand out by not exercising.

My father talked to the principal to have me formally excused from the exercises, and they agreed that it would be better if I just went straight to the classroom, rather than stand outside doing nothing while my classmates exercised. Then, when exercises were finished and everyone transitioned to the classroom, I would be present when classwork began. That is how I came to be alone in my sixth-grade classroom on the upper floor of the two-story Funairi Shogako (Funairi Elementary School) before classes began on August 6. It was my first day to skip the exercise period. It felt odd to be alone in the classroom. It was very quiet.

The hallways on each floor of our school building ran along the long side of the building. Large windows on one side of the hallway let in natural light from the outside, and classrooms were lined up along the other side of the hallway. The long wall between the hallway and the classrooms also had windows, so one could see outdoors from within the classrooms.

Seated at my desk and looking to the right I could see the beautiful blue sky through the two parallel walls with windows. It was still unusually bright and beautiful; the sky was blue, with no clouds. I had enjoyed the walk to school because it was such a beautiful morning and the sky was unusually clear and blue.

Flash!

I had been sitting quietly in the eerily still classroom admiring the pretty sky for about fifteen or twenty minutes when there was a bright flash. The flash was round, like a sun, the center was white, encircled by bright orange, and the outer edge around the circle was hot pink. It was startlingly bright; I dove to the floor, hurrying to seek shelter between desks, just as we had been taught: "Thumbs in ears, three fingers over eyes, pinkies hold nose, you can breathe through mouth." My side was still sore from the operation, and now I was a little bigger, a sixth grader. I couldn't quite fit under my desk, but I made myself as small as I could and crouched between two desks. Then I felt an unusual rumbling and the building began to shake. It wasn't like an earthquake, it was different, but I didn't know what it could be and thought I should leave the building. I looked to the right toward the hallway of windows, where I thought I would go to get out of the building. I started to rise from my space between the desks when the rumbling and shaking increased more and more. I thought, *oh my gosh!* and ducked back to my space between the desks. At the same time there was a big noise; the ceiling came crashing down. I was protected because although I was between the desks, I was crouched below the top surface of the desks. I felt a warm feeling on my back and my breath was taken away. It felt like my chest had been smashed. I didn't know why, and I didn't stop to think about it. There was so much commotion I just thought, *I need to get out of here*. It all happened fast, but I remember it clearly like it was yesterday.

I couldn't stand up because the ceiling was spread out across the tops of the desks, so I crawled out to the hallway, weaving my way between desks and under the ceiling. When I got to the hallway, I saw that the outside wall was gone, and the floor was completely covered with lumber, glass, and debris from the walls and Spanish-style tile roof. The stairs had disappeared under rubble. Material from the walls and ceiling covered the stairs and made it look like a giant slide. Broken glass was everywhere. I couldn't see the floor anywhere. I thought, *how am I going to get down?* As I went closer to where the stairs were, I saw that the outer wall of the staircase was also gone, but there were some narrow places along the inside wall where I could set my feet to make my way down. It was a slow process, but I made it to the ground floor.

Then I heard noises and children crying outside, and I thought I should find my shoes. In Hiroshima, most children wore geta, wooden sandals, but only while outside. Inside, we would store them in shoe racks and switch to indoor slippers. When I approached the shoe area, I found that the rack was toppled over, and some shoes were scattered nearby. But my shoes were not there; they must have been under the toppled rack, and that was too heavy for me to move.

I heard a male teacher outside call loudly, "Fifth and sixth-grade boys come and help!" I would later learn that one of the school walls fell on top of many of the lower grade students trapping them under it. But inside I did not know that; I was looking for my shoes and all the shoes were mixed up or under the heavy rack. I wasn't a fifth or sixth-grade boy, so I kept looking for my shoes. I heard crying. I thought, *forget the shoes, I need to get out of here,* and I ran out into the schoolyard wearing my indoor slippers. It was strangely dark outside, and I saw a few of my classmates on the far side of the schoolyard, so I ran toward them.

As I ran, one of my classmates exclaimed, "Where have you been?"

Another said, "Your back is bleeding!"

I told them I had been in the classroom, and I touched the back of my blouse and felt it was torn and damp. I wasn't thinking about that, though. No one knew what had happened.

The girl who noticed my bleeding back said, "We cannot go home now. We have to wait for roll call. The teacher said, 'Don't move.' We have to wait right here."

The teachers were all trying to free the younger students from under the wall. The unlucky class that had been exercising next to the school building was trapped under the wall. A few days later my father and I learned from the principal that over thirty students had been trapped under the wall and two had died. Later I heard that only two survived, but I don't know for certain.

Then, I saw my mother coming. I saw her at the gate of the school playground. Puff, puff, puff; she was running. I had never seen her run before. As she approached, I could see her face was red and puffy.

She said authoritatively, "You come home."

"No!" I cried. I would never disobey instructions from a teacher. I was thinking about the roll call.

"You come home with me," she insisted.

"No! I cannot. Teacher must have roll call," I insisted.

I was adamant, but she grabbed my hand and pulled me away. She said, "Roll call or no roll call, we're going home!" Some of the girls were trying to tell her that my back was bleeding, but she waved her other hand to quiet them and said something about "taking care of that," meaning my back. She held my hand all the way home, squeezing it so tightly it hurt. As we left the schoolyard, I saw piles of debris everywhere. Houses were flattened. And there were people on the ground everywhere asking for help or begging for water.

"What happened?" I asked. I couldn't make sense of what I was seeing. "What happened to her? What happened to them?"

My mother said the people got very hurt and she told me, "Don't look. Don't look." Again and again, "Don't look. Don't look."

She said they had been hurt too badly for us to help. I didn't realize they were burned. There were so many people.

I said, "They ask for water."

She said, "I know. Don't look."

She kept pulling me toward home. My hand hurt and it seemed everyone we saw was hurt.

When we did arrive home, it was pure shock to me. One wall was gone. The roof was gone. The door was torn down. There was glass and debris all over the floor. Our house was in shambles. Even the chaos I witnessed while rushing home didn't prepare me for seeing my house destroyed. Our beautifully kept home was truly destroyed. My mother walked straight into the ruins of our house, still holding my hand, and didn't even take off her shoes. She marched right across the delicate tatami mats, through the house and out to the backyard, pulling me along. We went through the backyard to where our bomb shelter was. Ours was the only one left standing in the neighborhood. Everyone else in our neighborhood had built their bomb shelters inside their houses, in a closet, and all the houses were demolished.

Chapter 7

Living in the Bomb Shelter

Confusion

We entered our bomb shelter. My hand was numb, and we were both short of breath. Our next-door neighbor, my mother's good friend, was there with the 3-year-old girl my mother had been watching that morning. Our next-door neighbor's whole face was burned, and her baby had died in the blast. She had been washing dishes near her kitchen window when the blast occurred. She saw the flash, her face suddenly felt hot, and she instinctively splashed water on it. She would survive, but her face took many months to heal, and the burns left her badly disfigured. Her bomb shelter was destroyed, so she stayed with us for several days. Since her husband was a contractor with Mitsubishi, he stayed at the plant like my father and some other employees did. Eventually, he and his wife moved north to Hokkaido, where she was originally from.

The toddler girl, the army officer's daughter, was unscathed. When the blast blew the roof off our house, my mother reflexively dived over the little girl and covered her with her own body. Mother suffered a deep gash on her head from falling debris, but she was very relieved the girl was unharmed. For many years after she expressed relief that the girl had not been hurt. She was worried about my back, though.

My father was at Mitsubishi when the bomb hit. People rushed to the Mitsubishi gate looking for medical attention, and many injured people flooded into the Mitsubishi clinic. The doctor realized they were not all company people, and that the clinic would not be able to help everyone, not even everyone who was under Mitsubishi's care.

My father's boss, the division president Mr. Niwa, called a meeting and said, "We got hit, but it doesn't look like a regular hit. Send someone to check on the town and find out what's going on out there."

No one thought anyone could get through the crowds at the gate.

Mr. Niwa, said, "If anyone can get through, it's Tajima."

So my father was sent with the company limousine. The limo only traveled a half block, and he reported back that he couldn't get through. Then he learned there had been a bomb, and he began to worry about home. He sent one of the workers by bicycle, through a side gate, to check on us. The worker found us in the bomb shelter and told us that Mr. Tajima was ok and wanted to know our condition.

My mother had already washed my back with water from the hibachi. She told the messenger that I was injured, showed him my burned back, and sent word that other than my injury, we were ok and were staying in the bomb shelter.

After receiving our message, my father immediately sent a company doctor from Mitsubishi by bicycle. The doctor came, carrying a black, old-fashioned doctor's bag, treated my back, and left a white, creamy ointment for me. He told my mother how to apply it and said he would return the next day.

My Father came home in the late afternoon to check on us. He had planned to return to work as quickly as possible, but at about that time, there was commotion in the neighborhood. Some neighbors who had stayed in the neighborhood were trying to clean up some of the debris. The army officer's wife had managed to walk home, looking for her three-year-old daughter who was with us. She collapsed in front of her house, a few houses down the street from ours.

One of the neighbors who lived about a block down the street from us came to our bomb shelter to say that the officer's wife had come back and had collapsed in front of her house. Those who saw her said she had walked slowly with her arms stretched out in front of her, and the skin of her arms and hands hung off her arms like dishcloths. At first, they thought she was walking with washcloths. She was looking for her three-year-old. She kept saying, "I looked everywhere, but I cannot find my baby." My mother went to her and told her that the older child was safe, with not one scratch on her. Then the woman lost consciousness.

Three neighbor men tried to carry her on a makeshift stretcher to the army clinic. Most people in the city then were old, because all the young men were serving in the war. My mother volunteered my father to help because the men were old and were having difficulty carrying her.

When my father saw the woman's condition, he said, "I'm not too sure . . .," thinking she would not survive.

My father was expected to go back to Mitsubishi after checking on me, but he helped carry her to the clinic. Later he saw her husband, the army officer. He told him that his daughter was unharmed and was with us in the bomb shelter. The officer came in the evening to get the little girl.

A few days later my mother and I walked to the Army hospital to see the woman before she died. Enemy planes flew over us many times, and we hid in the ditches by the road. People were lying about everywhere crying out, "Help, please!" My mother kept saying, "I'm sorry. I'm sorry." The people had lost their strength and could not even move anymore. They cried for water, but we were told that water wasn't good for them. My mother kept saying, I'm sorry! I'm sorry!" and tried to keep me from looking, but they were everywhere.

At the army camp, I could see our neighbor from the doorway. Later my mother said that her stomach had been bloated. She said, "thank you," to my mother for saving her little girl. She had only come back to her house for her little girl and was so glad she was ok. After she died, her husband, the army officer, became distraught. He asked my mother to take his daughter; he said he couldn't raise her by himself. The little girl stayed with us during the days while he worked. He wanted my parents to adopt her. My father said, "No, we don't know what is going to happen with the end of the war." At that time, we didn't know when or how the war would end, or what things would be like after the war. My mother convinced the soldier that the little girl needed him because he was her father, and eventually his parents came and took the little girl to care for her.

Returning to my demolished school

I was worried about missing classes, so I asked to go back to my school; I didn't want to fall behind. My mother said "no, not to that building." I asked three or four times saying that I at least wanted to get my textbooks. My father said he would take me, saying "ok, but maybe nobody will be there." He was right, no one was there when we arrived. When he saw the condition of the stairs, he was speechless.

He asked, "You were upstairs?"

"Yes."

"No one else was here?"

"No one."

And finally, "How did you come down?" he asked, almost with disbelief.

I scrambled up the debris to demonstrate, and he shook his head uncertainly. He expressed amazement that I was able to maneuver through the mess. He wasn't even sure he could climb up to the second floor, but I showed him where I had found places to step. It was trickier for him because his feet were bigger than mine. We made it to my classroom, and I showed him my classroom and my desk, and how I had followed procedure when the ground began rumbling. I crawled under the ceiling debris to my desk, showing him how I had crawled under the rubble, and then I retrieved my books and crawled back out. He was unusually quiet and kept shaking his head. We saw that there were a couple of heavy black roof tiles in the spot where I had been crouched between desks, and the ceiling debris had a big hole in it right there. My father said, "Oh, that's what hit you," referring to the roof tiles.

My black blouse had been burned and torn to shreds, but the white camisole underneath had only small brown burn spots. The black silk absorbed the heat, but the white cotton slip underneath saved my back. The difference in the condition of the fabrics is almost unbelievable. My mother kept the blouse and gave it to me when I left Japan, saying that I might like to keep it as a remembrance because it had been like a lucky charm for me. I have looked for it recently, but it is packed away in a moving box, and I haven't been able to find it yet.

My father looked around my classroom for a while, then we headed back to the ground level. Going down was even harder than going up, and I heard him say very quietly to himself, "You should have been a boy." I felt a little surge of pride that he was impressed I had managed it by myself.

Before leaving the school grounds, we saw the principal who had come to survey the damage. He was surprised to see us, and happy to see we were alive. We felt the same for him. He hadn't seen me at exercises on August 6, so he thought maybe I hadn't come to school that day. He didn't realize I had already gone to the classroom. I probably wasn't even missed at roll call. My father told him that we had come to get my books and they chatted for a bit. This is when we learned about the lower-grade class deaths. The news about the younger students was sad, but it was nice to see my principal was well. After our little visit, my father walked me home to the bomb shelter and then went back to Mitsubishi.

Doctor visits and uncertainty

From August 6 to August 17, mother and I lived in the bomb shelter, and the doctor who promised to return after the first day did return the next day, and the next day. He came every day by bicycle from Mitsubishi to check my burned back. There were so many others at Mitsubishi to care for, but he came to treat me every day. I was a lucky one, thanks to my father, and thanks to that doctor. He changed the dressings and reapplied the white ointment that had a distinctive odor.

My mother cooked on the shichirin, a Japanese cooking grill, in our backyard. She cooked for several families because many families lost their bomb shelters and stored supplies. We didn't eat the soybeans because there were enough provisions in the shelter, but the water was lifesaving, as she had predicted. The water pipe in the front yard broke and kept spewing water into the air. Until we left the shelter, we could still see fires at night. The sky was red in the direction of the city center, but we couldn't figure out why it was lasting so long. We thought surely the city couldn't still be burning. Later we were told that they were burning bodies.

Our next-door neighbor stayed three or four days; then her husband came to get her, and they found a place to live elsewhere on the outskirts of Hiroshima, where they stayed a while before moving to the northern island, Hokkaido. A couple of years later, while we were in Osaka, she invited my mother to Hokkaido for salmon season. I was in school and couldn't go, but my mother said the salmon up there "tastes so good," and she brought a big salmon home. My father never stayed in the shelter, but he checked in on us in the afternoons or sent someone to check if he was too busy. His decision to build our shelter the way he did, and my mother's foresight in stocking it gave us a safe place in all the chaos swirling around us at the time.

Chapter 8

Evacuation

End of war

On August 15, the emperor gave a speech. We had no radio in the bomb shelter, so my mother and I had no news. That afternoon, my father came to the shelter stern-faced and angry. He said, "They gave up. We promised to fight to the last man, but they gave up." I never saw him so angry. The emperor had accepted unconditional defeat. We had lost the war in an unimaginable manner. Before the surrender, the government had not told the public the state of the war, or that we were losing. Later my father told us that he had suspected that we were losing because ships were not returning to port for repairs. But giving up was a shock. We just quit as a nation, nowhere near fighting to the last man, and it was sickening to everyone.

My father worried that it would become unhealthy to remain in Hiroshima, but my mother did not want to leave our home, even though it was broken. We were making do in the shelter, and we had plenty of provisions. My parents argued about evacuating, but two days later, on August 17, my mother and I evacuated to the barn that had been prepared for us in the country. Father remained safe at Mitsubishi. He gave the ruins of our house and everything in it, including my sewing machine, to a young couple whose house had completely burned down.

To reach the barn, my father sent the company fire truck to our house. I was used to going to doctor appointments in the company car and wondered why there were no other vehicles except the fire truck. It was only two days after the war ended and already all other vehicles were unavailable. My mother gathered some items from the shelter: the two metal boxes of clothing, a few kitchen items, both hibachi; and then we left on the fire truck. Everywhere, people were walking away from the city; everyone asked for a ride.

The driver said, "No."

My mother said, "ok."

More and more people begged to catch a ride. "One more! Please, one more!"

Mother felt sorry for them all and said "yes" to everyone. People were hanging onto the sides of the truck. The driver warned her that the truck wasn't made for this and that we were carrying too much weight.

He kept saying, "Mrs. Tajima, this vehicle is not made to take this heavy load. We cannot carry this much weight."

When we passed by broken streetcars, I saw the charcoal people. They looked like shadows, like ghosts, only dark. I asked my mother who they were, and she said, "Don't look, don't look." She kept repeating, "Don't look. Don't look." But I had already looked. It looked like people were holding on to the hand bars on the streetcars, or waving at others, but they weren't moving. In other places, it looked like people were sitting on the ground, but they were motionless.

"It looks like people are still standing there," I said.

"No. I think it's just shadows," she said. She didn't want me to see the charcoal people.

It was eerie, but I didn't know what I was seeing. Even today it seems incredible to me that those charcoal figures had been alive and doing ordinary daily activities, then in a moment they were all dead, still upright, seemingly frozen in time but actually burnt to a crisp. We chugged along past the city, and just outside the city, the truck broke down. We walked to the nearest farmhouse, and the farmer and his wife kindly invited us to stay for dinner. My mother and I ate dinner there at the farmhouse, and the poor driver walked all the way back to Mitsubishi to report what had happened. He was given tools and parts to repair the fire truck.

The next morning, he arrived with the tools and parts. After making the repairs, he drove us the rest of the way to the barn. He unloaded our belongings into the barn and then took the fire truck back to Mitsubishi. The next day my father came. He was angry because of why the fire truck had broken and because the episode had caused great difficulty for the driver.

"Why did it break?" he asked my mother.

"I think it was a little overloaded," she said.

"Why overloaded?" he asked.

She said nothing, but my father knew. My mother couldn't say no to anyone.

The kamikaze pilot that didn't die

Everybody has a crazy cousin, and mine was Shigeru. He was a few years older than me, but not yet old enough to join the military. Early in the war, my mother and I had gone to the port in Kobe to see his two older brothers, Noburu and Mori, depart for duty after they had been drafted. Shigeru's parents weren't happy about that, but they were relieved that at least their third son was too young to be drafted. But Shigeru wanted to fight for Japan so badly he forged papers to join a kamikaze unit. He and his family were living in Korea at the time, and when military recruiters came to his high school to draft volunteers, he signed up and forged his parents' signatures on the consent papers.

He was immediately shipped off to training near Tokyo. The principal of the school saw Shigeru's name on the military's list of draftees and thought it unlikely that the Kijima family would allow Shigeru to join the military as a draftee. The principal knew that the Kijima family put education first and would have expected Shigeru to go to college, just as his two older brothers had done. He contacted Shigeru's parents to see if they had truly given consent.

Mr. and Mrs. Kijima were alarmed to learn what their son had done, and they tried to have his enlistment nullified because their signatures had been forged and he was underage. They were unsuccessful (we thought it was because the military was desperate for volunteers at that time), and Shigeru was allowed to continue training through to completion.

When his number came up to fly, he was celebrated and toasted to the night before his scheduled flight, as was done for every kamikaze pilot. His whole family was sad. My mother was so, so sad. But the next day he didn't get to fly because the war effort was called off. He was released from service.

He thought he could try to find his uncle, my father, so he boarded a train to Hiroshima. When he got off the train, he saw the flattened landscape. He turned around and got right back on the train, thinking his uncle must be dead because no one could have survived that.

His next thought was to return to Korea, where his family had been living. Many people told him that all Japanese families had left Korea, but he didn't think that could be correct; so he took a train to the sea, boarded a ferry, and crossed the water to Korea. When he finally arrived in Korea, he found that like most Japanese, they indeed had left Korea, and he had no idea where they were. A friend helped him secure a ticket for a ferry back to Japan because by now he had little money.

He then went back to Hiroshima to see if he could learn anything at Mitsubishi about his uncle's family, my family. There he learned that Mr. Tajima had in fact survived. By then, Father had heard from his sister, Shigeru's mother. She said they had survived and had settled in a quiet area north of Tokyo. He had their address and was able to put Shigeru on the path home.

Living in the country barn house

My mother and I stayed at the barn until January. The accommodations were pleasant considering the circumstances. The spaces were nicely finished, and the rooms were comfortable. One room had a large picture window looking out to the beach. Downstairs was a grill and a well with a hand pump. The farmer brought fresh food to us every day while we were there. I remember the peaches and tangerines were especially delicious. My mother cooked on the grill downstairs. Father checked in on us sometimes. The doctor continued to visit me by bicycle every day. He biked all the way from Mitsubishi to the country barn to check my burns. We called them "stubborn burns" because they refused to heal, and I became impatient with them.

The farmer and his wife were kind to us, but I was anxious to get back to school. Since I was in sixth grade, I was supposed to be preparing for high school entrance exams. I had my heart set on one school, Ichijo. It was the top-rated school in Hiroshima. Competition for a slot in that school was tough, but I had wanted to go there ever since I had first learned about it. The academic instruction there was very good, and being a serious student, I wanted to go there.

The end-of-year term, January through mid-March, was traditionally the time sixth graders prepare for high school entrance examinations. Teachers help students with academic material and practice interviews. Some children, especially those living in rural areas, go to prep school or trade school instead of competing for high school. But I was a city girl, and I wanted to attend Ichijo. My father found an empty house south of all the destruction and arranged for us to move into it.

Hiroshima Key Locations

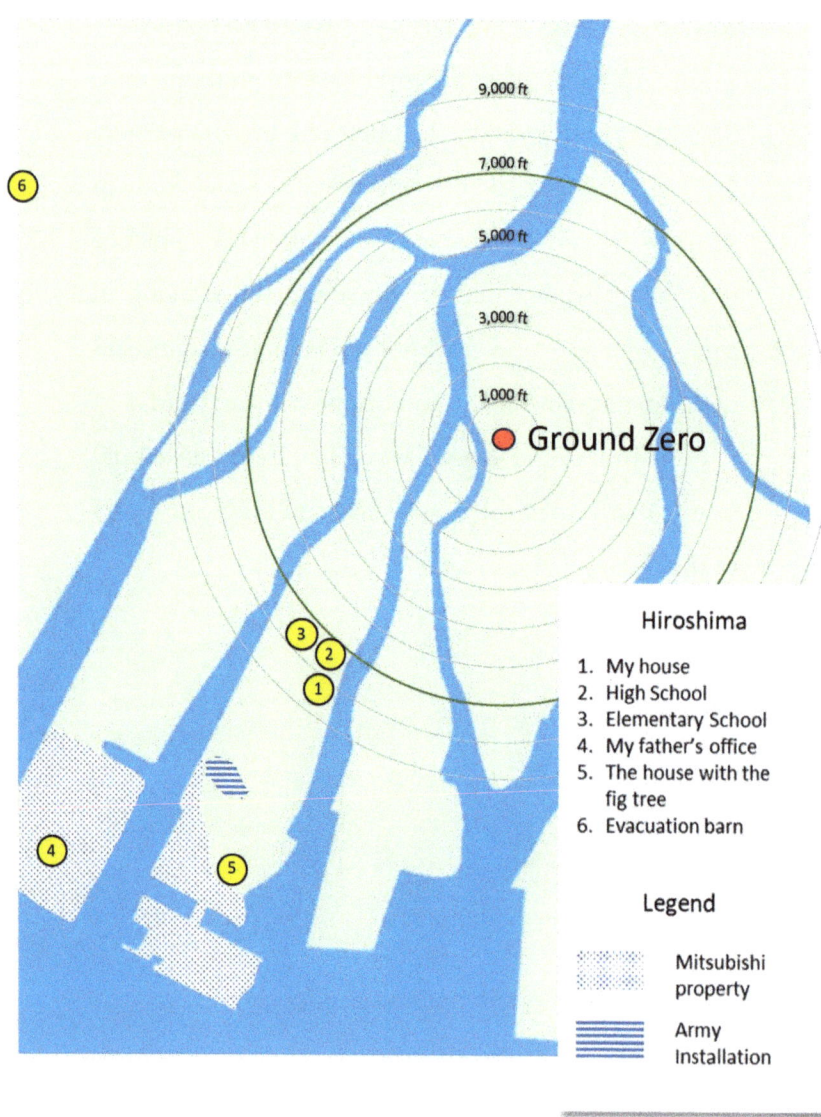

9,000 ft
7,000 ft
5,000 ft
3,000 ft
1,000 ft

● Ground Zero

Hiroshima

1. My house
2. High School
3. Elementary School
4. My father's office
5. The house with the fig tree
6. Evacuation barn

Legend

Mitsubishi property

Army Installation

I was standing next to some women from my mother's club who supported young military members and their families. After the war, my mother cut away and burned the image of the ladies to avoid possible accusations of complicity.

Here I was standing next to a Japanese Navy officer, the brother of the army officer whose daughter stayed with me in the shelter. My mother cut away and burned all images that linked us to the war. Hiroshima, Feb 4, 1945.

My mother refreshed the water in this colorful hibachi daily until the bomb fell. Everyday she said repeatedly, "we will use this someday. This will be a lifesaver someday," as she worked to change the water. She was proven correct.

My father commissioned a metalworker to craft these two metal cans so we could store clothing in the bomb shelter and evacuation location.

Places of Interest in Japan

Part III

Occupation

Chapter 9

Return to Hiroshima

Country House South of Eba

The house we moved into was a large family home with a big fig tree in the front yard. It was one of three large country houses south of the Eba area near the army installation. A widow lived in the middle house, a fisherman lived next to her, and we lived on the other side. The fisherman and my mother knew one another from before the end of the war. He had learned that she appreciated the best of the catch, and they had developed a friendly business relationship. During those days, he even brought fresh fish to our house and cleaned and fileted them for her outside, near our kitchen door.

After the war ended, seafood became harder to obtain. But living near the fisherman was nice because we were at least able to get nori (seaweed) easily. There

I saw how the seaweed was processed. The fisherman brought it ashore, rinsed it with clean water repeatedly, and then spread it onto screens in individual, thin, square portions to dry in the sun. I learned about fisherman's lunch from him, too. It needs no refrigeration and is simple to prepare, consisting of a pickled plum buried in a ball of rice sprinkled with soy sauce or salt and sesame seeds and wrapped with nori. It is economical, fortifying, and delicious, and I still enjoy them today.

Other things were harder to find. My mother bought Hershey's chocolate off the black market for me. I didn't realize how special it was until I heard a neighbor exclaim, "Oh, that's so expensive!" and my mother responded, "But she likes it."

Classes resume

The building was only half standing, and the books and school supplies were gone, but we had school. The teachers and school administrators made makeshift study materials. They wrote out information we might have learned from textbooks and fashioned a sort of homemade book for each of us to study. It was an important year for us to complete, because right after 6th grade came high school entrance examinations. Those exams determined where one would go to school for the next five years. At that time, schools were not coed past 6th grade, and students had to take entrance examinations and interview to be admitted to the better high schools.

The top-rated and most prestigious schools' tests were the first to be administered. A week or so later, second-tier schools administered their tests. This gave students a chance to apply to a top school if they wanted to, but still have an opportunity to test elsewhere if they failed to be admitted to the top school. I grew more and more nervous about those exams. I said that if I didn't get into my dream school, I would not test for a second-tier school the following week. Then, I said I would kill myself.

Entrance Exam and Surviving Sisters

Finally, in the spring, it was time to test for high school admission. A dozen of my classmates from Funairi

Shogako and many students from other schools applied to Ichijo. The teachers at our elementary school went to different high schools to chaperone during the testing. There weren't enough teachers to cover all the schools, so my father was asked to chaperone at Ichijo.

The first test covered two subjects: moral education and reading. We had breaks between sections and were allowed to go outside to relax for a few minutes. During the first break, one girl said loudly, "Have you heard? This school is going to automatically admit any girl who had a sister at this school that died in the bombing." I froze. Many girls from Ichijo had died in the bombing. How many had sisters? I felt sick with worry and started to approach my father. He had heard the girl and immediately told me not to worry and to do my best. I worried anyway. The next test was the math exam. There were only two problems, which made the test seem even worse because to miss one would result in a 50%. Certainly, that was true for everyone taking the test, but to look at the page containing only two problems was unnerving to me. Somehow, I managed to get through the exams and then started the other nerve-wracking part: waiting for the results.

Waiting for test results

For days I was scared I wouldn't be accepted. I continued saying that if I didn't get into my dream school, I would not test for a second-tier school the following week, that I would kill myself! Those few days before the results were published were agonizing. On the day they were supposed to be posted, I was too nervous to go to the school to check the results, so that morning I asked my father to check for me. I knew this meant I would have to wait until he came home from work, but I was too nervous to go myself. I spent the whole day feeling sick with anxiety.

Finally, the end of the day arrived, but then my father wasn't home at his regular time. I realized that he had to travel to the school before coming home, which took an additional hour of commuting time. When he did finally come in, he was very quiet. Naturally, I thought the silence meant that I had failed, and he was disappointed in me. Wordlessly, he took off

97

his shoes and hung his coat while I was right there in front of him. I was so afraid to ask, but finally I did. I asked him if he had gone by the school. He looked at me and simply said "Yes."

After a long, sickening pause, he quietly asked, "Kazuko, do you remember you said that if you were not admitted you would kill yourself?"

I remember struggling to verbalize, "Yes."

He said, "Well, you don't have to do it."

I have never been so relieved and exhausted at the same time, and I'm sure I slept well that night.

High School at Ichijo

Shortly after the first term began in April, we took a class photo. Normally one would see all the students wearing the school uniform, but uniforms were unavailable at that time. There were few school supplies, only makeshift books, and no uniforms after the bombing. Yet in the photo all but four students, me and three other girls, had uniforms. Many girls wore their sister's uniform. I was thrilled to have made it into one of the remaining slots, but then equally disappointed by the next turn of events. After all the effort and anxiety leading up to high school admission, I only attended Ichijo for three months, April, May, and June. And then, my father was transferred yet again.

Chapter 10

Goodbye Hiroshima, Hello Kyoto and Osaka

Father transfers to Kyoto and Osaka

I mmediately after the war, the new government wanted to break up all companies that had a wartime role. At the same time, the Mitsubishi plant in Kyoto was having a hard time transitioning from war to business production. Their wartime role was building airplanes, and they were struggling to find a new role. So, Mitsubishi sent my father to Kyoto. I didn't like that at all. He had always helped me with homework after school, but since he was so far away, I had to rely on my mother for help. My mother was well-educated; she had attended Ozuma, a special finishing school. She was well known for being a creative cook; she was always the first to deliver home-cooked meals to anyone in need. She was an elegant hostess; she set out the loveliest tea spread and light dinners for entertaining my father's co-workers many times a week. She was clever and resourceful in obtaining supplies during and after the war. However, her teaching style went something like this: "I showed you how to do that. Why don't you understand?" Oh, how I missed my father! My mother hired a tutor who was a few years older than me, and she came to help me sometimes. Despite all the changes we were making things work.

By this time, the U.S. was beginning to transform our way of life. Eventually, our holidays, celebrations, lifestyle, and educational system all were impacted. My father had warned that changes would come, but immediately after the war ended, we didn't know what those changes would be. One day my mother visited people dear to her in Tokyo and returned in tears and was nearly inconsolable because of the way they were living. Americans had taken over their residences and they were living in the servants' quarters.

My mother worried that families who had links to the war effort might be singled out by the

Americans. She decided to eliminate anything in our possession that might be incriminatory. My photo album was like a scrapbook, with photos pasted onto the pages. She carefully peeled away photos that she thought might jeopardize our safety, including those that showed her with women's groups involved in supporting newly drafted and recruited military members and those showing anyone in uniform. There was one photo of me with a Japanese naval officer, the uncle of the little girl who stayed with us in the shelter. She liked that photo, so she didn't peel away the whole picture. She neatly trimmed away the officer and left me standing by myself next to a scarred bit of scrapbook page. Then she gathered all those possibly incriminatory photos and papers together and burned them.

Meanwhile, in Kyoto, my father was very busy trying to minimize losses as the division closed plane-building operations. Soon it became clear that the division in Osaka also desperately needed leadership help. My father went there, too. He commuted back and forth between the two cities, trying to keep them both afloat. During that time, he held two positions:

vice president and CEO. I missed him so much, but I was proud of him.

After my first term at Ichijo ended, my mother and I moved to Kyoto to be with my father. Poof! That was the end of my dream school. We knew the stay in Kyoto would be short, so we stayed in a Mitsubishi family dormitory. I expected to have to take another school entrance exam, but the principal of my new school, Funi Koto Jogako, knew of Ichijo's reputation and waived it for me. Kyoto was the only major city spared from the bombings, so the schools there had not experienced as many wartime interruptions and were academically ahead of schools elsewhere. The city was still pristine and beautiful. The textbooks were real, not in-house makeshift books, and the school building was still standing. It was much different from where we had just been.

We stayed in Kyoto for three months, with my father commuting back and forth to Osaka the whole time. Then, before the winter term began, the three of us moved together to Osaka where I finished my first year of high school at Osaka Fu Neyagawa Koto Jogako. I had attended three different schools that year. My new home was far from school, so I learned to use the train system.

Osaka

While in Osaka, my father led Mitsubishi's efforts there to survive in the aftermath of the war. We lived in the back of a small retail shop that my father had built with the intention of turning it into a marketplace for the local Kyoto-Osaka-Kobe area. The Kyoto-Osaka-Kobe area was, and still is, referred to as Kinki. The shop was a Kinki Store, which was a chain of well-known local specialty stores at the time. I now know that "kinki" sounds humorous to western ears, so when I say that I lived in the back of a Kinki store, I have some explaining to do! While revising this book, Kinki University changed its name to Kindai University specifically to avoid the snickering they encountered at international gatherings. Funny name aside, the store was an effort to help Mitsubishi transition away from wartime activities. It was designed with one area for a retail shop, one area for a coffee shop, and a living space in the back. They made novelty trinkets to sell and brainstormed way outside their usual area of business. They tried to help Mitsubishi and the local citizens survive in the lean times by experimenting with preserving foods and designing useful objects using leftover wartime materials.

I remember they crafted heavy ashtrays and a small charcoal-burning room heater out of metals and parts no longer used to make airplanes to sell in the shop. Even my mother helped in the effort by finding ways to use dried foods: apples, bananas, onions, potatoes, yellow chrysanthemums, and many other things. Dried mums aren't tasty, so she pickled them with sweet vinegar. Some efforts were successful, others not so much. My father's brother-in-law, Mr. Kijima, said he would help run the shop while my father worked at Mitsubishi. My father built a small house for him next to the store, and they and their two youngest children, including Shigeru, moved into it.

Completing High School

After the war, high schools were converted to coed. This happened at my school during my third year of high school. To achieve the mixing that the Americans wanted us to have, some boys from boys' schools were sent to girls' schools, and some girls from girls' schools were sent to boys' schools. In my case, I stayed in my girls' school in Osaka, and some boys came from elsewhere to study with us. Nobody liked that. The boys especially hated being in a school meant to be for girls. It was humiliating for them. They snickered or made derisive noises anytime a girl made a mistake. We girls thought it was a little invasive to have boys in our school. Some girls were intimidated into keeping quiet or not participating in class discussions. But we had lost the war, and these changes were another part of the sting of it.

Since we now had boys in our class, physical education class was different, too. We played softball sometimes. The first time we played, I didn't know much about the game. I probably should have known at least a little because my father was a baseball player. He had played for his company teams at the power company and at Mitsubishi. I had been to his company baseball games and had seen him pitch, but I had not paid enough attention to the game itself to know the rules. I was always happy when my father's team won, but I never paid any attention to how it had happened.

Before we played our first softball game during PE class, I think surely the teacher must have explained the rules, but evidently, I didn't pay attention to the instructions. On my first turn at bat, I stepped up to home plate. I did at least know I should swing at the ball. When the ball came towards me, I swung the bat. Bang! The sound surprised me. I stood there, surprised. Then I heard loud clapping and hollering, "Run! Run! Run! Run!" I looked around and saw people waving their arms and shouting, "Run! Run!" so I started running. I ran all the way to first base. There I stopped. But people were still clapping and were now pointing at second base and hollering at me to keep running. So, I ran to second base. And still they were clapping and hollering, and they pointed me on to third base! I was a fast runner for short distances, and by now I was winded, but they kept hollering so I kept running, on to third base, past third base and on to home plate. When my father came home that evening, I told him about it. Smiling broadly, he said, "You made a home run." He was so proud! My mother, of course, thought girls didn't need to do such things, but I was happy my father enjoyed my home run!

He was my number one fan, but he also enjoyed having pleasant, mentoring conversations with other young people. He was interested in different subjects and different cultures and thought people can learn from others by simply listening. I remember him criticizing the business mentality of ignoring engineers because they didn't have a business background. He thought engineers could have good ideas, too, and he was willing to at least listen to their ideas. There were several young college students in Osaka who spent time at our house conversing with my father. They had varying interests and majors: agriculture, education, and others. One college boy who had lost both his parents looked to my father for advice regarding his future. He lived nearby with his sister in the house that had belonged to their parents, and they had a piano.

I was still thinking it would be nice to learn to play piano, and when he learned that about me, he offered to let me use theirs for practice. My father didn't know that my grades were slipping a bit at the time, and I was set up with lessons with a teacher who lived not too far away. Finally, my piano dream was coming true. I had lessons at the teacher's house, I practiced at the college student's house, and my grades continued to hover below my best.

When my father saw that my grades were not as good as they had been, he issued a warning, telling me to raise my grades or "you will have to stop piano." I didn't think he would do that. He was the papa who bought every toy sold in the novelty shops for me when I was younger, in Kobe. Granted, these were not Toys-R-Us type stores, but when a family friend in Kobe took me to a shop, wanting to buy me a toy, I couldn't find a single toy that I didn't already have. When Papa ran out of toys to buy me, he brought home colored pencils. School came first, though, even after the war, and he wasn't lenient when my grades dropped. He surprised me when he followed through and made me stop piano lessons.

My last years of schooling were not what I had prepared for in elementary school. Part way into my high school years, high schools transitioned to coed and were shortened from five to three years, and three-year junior high schools were formed. Even the names of schools were changed. School uniforms were replaced by the requirement to wear navy and white clothing, although most students continued to wear some sort of school uniform, even if it was from a different school. In Osaka, I wore an older friend's uniform from another school when she outgrew it. General MacArthur "suggested" many changes that westernized our culture, and our government followed his suggestions. My dream school and all that it represented to me was part of my past. When I was ready to graduate from high school, my father gave me a choice: I could go on to college or get a job. He said that if I had been a boy, he would not give me the choice; he would have required me to go to college. I chose to stop schooling. I took jobs working with Americans. I think my father felt that Japan wasn't Japan anymore, that it was changing so much and so fast that my future, and our nation's future, was no longer clear. The Americans were the winners, and we adjusted to a new reality.

Chapter 11

Meeting Americans

Job search

During my last term of high school, classmates often mentioned my good fortune in not having to worry about finding a job after graduation. It was presumed that I would be able to work at Mitsubishi.

Classmates said, "Oh, you're so lucky, you don't have to worry," so often that I didn't think much about my future. But when I asked my father about working at Mitsubishi, he simply said, "no." I was surprised and a bit miffed. Much later he explained that he had thought that I wouldn't learn anything if I worked there because everyone in the office would try to do all my work for me. But at the time, I was annoyed with him.

With the plan of working at Mitsubishi dashed, I scrambled to come up with a new plan. I enrolled in typing school thinking I could learn a marketable skill. During that time, my cousin Noburu, was working as a writer in the Japanese movie industry. One day he came to my home and told my mother that there was a role that was perfect for me.

He said, "This role is just made for Kazuko. She can do it. I know it."

He knew the director and seemed certain I would get the role. My mother didn't think it was a bad idea. She had known for some time that I didn't suffer from stage fright. I think most people knew I was ok with being onstage. Before my first performance in a play during first grade, I remember a lady backstage telling me not to be afraid and that when looking out to the audience it would be dark, that I wouldn't be able to see people's eyes. She said that over and over, so I wouldn't be scared. But when I went onstage and looked out to the audience, I did see their eyes. But it didn't bother me at all. I wondered what the lady had been talking about.

So, when Noburu offered to set up an appointment for me to meet the Japanese movie director, my mother agreed. This sounded good to me, better than typing class.

The morning of my appointment, my father happened to be home. He saw me dressed for the interview and preparing to leave home with Noburu, and he exclaimed, "Oh! Where are you going?"

Knowing that he would probably not approve of the meeting, my mother tried to smooth over the situation and explained that Noburu had kindly set up an interview for me. After a, "What are you talking about?" from my father, and additional smooth talking by my mother, my father exploded, "My daughter is not going to be an entertainer!"

I thought, *what's wrong with being an entertainer? He has friends who are entertainers. What's wrong with that?* But that was the end of that. My acting career was over!

So, I finished typing school. I managed to reach a respectable 67 words per minute by graduation, and then I was told that to be employed as a typist in Japan, I would have to work one full year with no pay. That seemed like a foolish thing to do; I wasn't going to do that! So, I started looking for yet another option for work. My mother knew someone who knew someone in the employment office at Itami Air Base, and he convinced my mother that I would be safe working in the Special Services office there. The office was located just inside the gate, and the work was simple office work, mostly handing out tickets for special events. Itami Air Base was on the opposite side of Osaka from my home, so I could get there by train. The commute took a couple of connections, but my mother waited for me at the train station nearest our home after work every day. My father didn't know about this plan until I had been hired and was already working.

Working girl

Special Services was in the same building as the snack bar, and on my first day of work there, one of the sergeants from the snack bar appeared at noon and bellowed, "How many of you want lunch?" All the other girls raised their hands, hopped up and hurried after him singing out, "I do!" One of the girls grabbed my hand and raised it into the air, then said, "come on!" I was going to eat a lunch I had brought from home, a lunch that my mother had made for me, but she said, "no! Just leave it there! Come on!" pulling me along with her. So, I hurried along with the other girls. As we settled along the counter in our break room, I learned that lunch was a hamburger with French fries and Coca-Cola. I had never had a hamburger before, and I soon realized why the other girls were so excited about lunchtime. It was good! The same thing happened the next day, and then the next day, too. That was our lunch every day for the whole time that I worked there! I had taken my homemade lunch back home after the first day, telling my mother that I wouldn't need lunches because they fed us at work. When she learned that the lunch was hamburger, French fries, and Coca-Cola, she was surprised and expected that I would tire of them quickly. I am still amazed that I never got tired of them.

At the end of the day, we were supposed to mop the floors. I knew about cleaning floors because Japanese students cleaned classroom floors at the end of every school day, but these mops were different.

They were huge, and I couldn't manage them very well. Everyone laughed when they saw me trying to mop the floors, and someone always shouted out, "Move over, I'll take over!" and took the mop from me. It was a jovial atmosphere. I was learning that the Americans were fun to be around.

Once, one of my friends wanted to go to the Osaka train station to see her American G.I. boyfriend off because he had orders to leave Japan. This large station was located across from Mitsubishi's office where my father worked, and it was on my route home. She didn't want to go by herself, so I went with her, without informing my parents. I was late getting home, but my mother was still at the train station waiting for me when I arrived. She was not upset with me, but when we finally made it home, my father was angry. He was angry at me for having stopped at the Osaka train station to see the G.I.s off. At the time I didn't think it was such a bad thing, but now I think he may have been embarrassed that someone from work might have seen me waving good-bye to uniformed GIs.

I worked at Special Services for just a few months until the office closed. Itami Air Base was undergoing changes because the Korean War had started. U.S. Air Force personnel moved away toward Korea and were replaced by U.S. Marines. When the Air Force's Special Services office closed, I returned to the employment office to apply for a new position.

Just as I entered the office, the Air Force mess sergeant, the person in charge of the dining facility, saw me and asked if I was looking for a job. When I affirmed that I was, he said, "Come with me!" and told the employment officials, "She's working for me!" and off we went.

Itami had four or five Marine dining facilities, which we called mess halls, and only one Air Force mess hall at the time. The Air Force mess sergeant wasn't happy that he kept losing space to the Marines as the Air Force-Marine balance on base shifted.

We girls were not supposed to date the men we met at work, but many did, and I did, too. When the mess sergeant learned that I had gone out with the Marine in charge of the Marine mess halls, he got angry about it. When I arrived at work, one of my friends warned me that he was very angry.

I said, "Oh, that's ok. I quit." I thought if he was so angry at me, I would just quit.

She couldn't believe I was saying that or that I would do that. I told her to tell the mess sergeant that I quit, and I turned around and went back to the employment office.

During the occupation, many Americans employed Japanese girls to help with housework and childcare duties. The girls who were allowed to work on base didn't always have the skills or background for such work, but we had a respectable education and English-speaking skills, and we came from good homes. I was offered a job working for Lt. White and his wife, who were just arriving from the States. I didn't have housekeeping skills, but I was assured that another girl, Betti, would do the housekeeping, and I only had to watch the children.

When I entered the White's house on my first day of work, Betti had already washed all the glasses and dishes and had put them in the cupboard. I helped her check that everything was clean and stored neatly. I thought I might learn some housekeeping skills from her.

Then Mrs. White arrived. She walked into the kitchen, picked up a glass from the shelf, and held it up high, turning it round to inspect it. Then she began pulling everything out of the cupboards and began washing without acknowledging our presence.

Betti said, "Ma'am, these have already been washed."

Mrs. White ignored her and continued washing while Betti and I stood by and watched silently. Mrs. White's manner made Betti so angry that she left the house and didn't come back. The next two days were the weekend, and when Monday arrived, she still hadn't come back. She just quit. I was employed there for three or four weeks, doing nothing but watching their children. Then the Whites were reassigned to another military installation in northern Japan.

After the Whites transferred out, I moved to Lt James' house. His wife was nice. There was another girl who was already doing the housekeeping, so I watched their children. I had grown up as an only child, so it was interesting to watch children play together under one roof, and I enjoyed playing with them, too. It was a pleasant household, but I wasn't there for very long. The Jameses were also transferred to northern Japan, although they didn't seem to want to go there.

When they left, I went to the employment office again. While I was waiting to be helped, my old boss, the Air Force mess sergeant, walked in and saw me.

He said, "What are you waiting for? Are you looking for another job?"

I replied that I was, and he said that I could work for him at his house. There was no mention of my walking out of the mess hall job. I had some doubts about working for him, but for the second time, I followed him out of the employment office to work for him.

He lived in the Takarazuka area, where the houses are huge, and the properties are surrounded by high walls with tall iron gates. His son's name was Butchie, and my job was to watch him. We played, and I prepared his breakfast and peeled grapefruits for him. His parents thought I was spoiling him, because of the way I peeled the fruit. I didn't know of any other way to serve grapefruit, and when I learned the method of cutting grapefruit in half and eating it with a spoon, I thought it seemed odd, but of course I didn't say so.

Butchie's mother did sewing by hand, and I learned a lot from her. She bought fabric from the post exchange store and made a dress by hand. When I told her that it looked nice, she showed me how she made it and bought fabric for me. She was kind.

When they were transferred back to the States, I went to work at Sgt Seagriss's house. His wife was an alcoholic, and I don't think she was ever sober. She didn't do anything around the house; the sergeant did it all. I learned to prepare some American snacks from him. His wife was so drunk most of the time that he prepared the meals. Once, he cooked frog legs and told his wife not to tell me what they were. After we ate, they asked me what I thought of them, and I said that I thought they were pretty good. I thought they were chicken legs.

Then they told me, "You just ate frog legs!" They thought it was funny. Really funny.

I've made some of his snacks over the years, but never the frog legs.

One weekend, I went home to celebrate my birthday with my family. Sgt Seagriss gave me a beautifully decorated birthday cake to take home. It was a big cake and difficult to carry on the train, but it was nice of him. Someone told his wife that he had given me the cake, and when I returned after the weekend, she had already hired a new girl to help in the house. When I arrived, the new girl was wearing my clothes. She said that Mrs. Seagriss had given all my clothes to her, insisting that she wear them. I retrieved my clothes, including the ones the girl was wearing, and I left the Seagrisses.

A little while later, Sgt Seagriss called my mother and told her that he wanted to see me. I met him after work, and he told me that he had sent his wife back to the States and apologized for her behavior. He was being transferred to western Japan, and he wanted me to go with him. I thanked him and wished him luck but didn't go with him. I sometimes wonder how things went for him. I hope well.

By then, three or four of my friends had moved to Oppama, near the naval base in Yokosuka. They had traveled to Yokosuka to say good-bye to their boyfriends who shipped out from the port there. After their boyfriends left, they took jobs at the Enlisted Men's (EM) club. They liked working there and convinced me to join them. I rented a room nearby, in Oppama, and went to work at the EM Club. The EM Club was a huge building previously used by the Japanese Navy officers and contained a ship store, movie theater, dance floor, the Top Three Club, three or four large rooms for hosting parties, and a very good snack bar. It was the place to order the nicest cakes, impressively decorated and tasty, too. I worked at the Top Three Club, the club for chiefs and first- and second-class chief petty officers. It was a good time.

The girls told me right away that although I used my real name to apply for the job, I should not use my real name while at work. Sailors often went to the employment office to find out where a girl lived, and then they would show up unannounced at her home. I took their advice, and I went by the name Machiko. Another girl, Kayoko, turned out to be Sumi, and we became good friends later when we lived in the United States.

125

One day the employment officer, a Japanese civilian, called me to his office and wanted to know if I was telling people that my name was Machiko. Evidently a sailor had gone to him and asked for Machiko's address. He told the sailor that there was no one by that name working at the club. The sailor proceeded to describe me, and the employment officer realized it was me. He told the sailor my real name, and then he sent for me. He wanted to know why I was not using my real name.

I said, "Well, if I tell the sailors my real name, they will come here and ask you for my address."

He said, "Yes. So what?"

I said, "Then you will give it to them, right?"

He said, "Yes, so what?

I said, "Well that's why. I don't want them knocking at my door."

Then he understood and replied, "Oh."

And then, of course, the sailor did show up at my home. But it was a wasted trip for him.

Al

I saw U.S. Navy Chief Petty Officer Albert Blake from a distance several times before I met him. I used to see him chatting with some of my friends. After I met him, he asked me out once or twice, but I said no. Then Holiday on Ice came to Japan. It seemed that everyone was talking about how spectacular it was, but I hadn't seen it. Friends had invited me to go with them, but something always came up and I couldn't go. Even my mother and her friends had seen it. Then Al asked me in the nicest manner if I would accompany him to see it on his birthday. He said that the Ice Capades were better, but Holiday on Ice was still a good show. Somehow, he didn't speak like the others there, and his manner caught my attention. I said yes. Turned out, he was a pretty nice guy. We dated for quite a while before jumping through many, many governmental hoops to marry.

After getting married, my friend, Kabaya-san, gave me a gold piece and said that if "something" were to happen, I was to make my way to the coast, and we would "figure it out from there." I had no intention of leaving Japan, but she was kind to look after me in that way.

Al was able to get his tour extended, and we rented a house in Oppama for a year after the wedding. I learned Japanese dance and became certified in Ikebana, Japanese flower arranging. My mother helped make that happen, thinking I should have certified skills. I think she was still protecting me.

Most of our friends were shipped back to the U.S., but I naively thought that Al would stay in Japan. I thought he would get a job in Japan and stay. Some others had done that. But, alas, he received orders to Washington, D.C., and we began planning to ship out like our friends had done. I kept thinking that it wouldn't really happen, that we wouldn't really leave Japan.

Eventually the day did come for us to leave. It was the day before my birthday. I was very unhappy. I didn't want to leave Japan, and I certainly didn't want to spend my birthday, the next day, on the sea, far from my family and friends.

Chapter 12

Goodbye Japan

I don't think many other girls left Japan with the feelings I had. I didn't view it as an exciting adventure. Later, after arriving in the States, there would be much adventure, and within a few years I became a U.S. citizen. I adopted the U.S. as my new country, of course. But that August day in 1957 was not a happy day for me.

My mother and many friends came to the port to see us off. They were allowed to board the U.S. Navy ship and visit for about twenty or thirty minutes. Military bases restrict entry, so we felt fortunate that they were allowed to come aboard with us.

Shortly before our departure, my mother said, "I have the feeling that this is the last time I will see you."

Surprised, I replied quickly and confidently, "No! I'll be back within two years!"

Maybe I was thinking that Al's assignment would last about two years, and then we could return to Japan on his next assignment. The words just popped out. And then, too soon, it was time for her and my friends to leave the ship and depart the base. In the end, she was correct, as she so often was. I didn't return and she died several years later. I remember waving to them from the deck of the ship. By then my feelings had boiled into anger. I did not want to leave Japan.

We were supposed to sail to San Francisco, California, but the ship was diverted to Seattle, Washington. We stopped briefly in Hawaii, where Al was able to send a message to his parents, who had planned to meet us in San Francisco. The trip itself was nice for a military ship, because Al and I had our own cabin. All the other couples were crammed into cabins: four wives to a room, and four men to a room. The lower area of the ship carried many Marines returning from Korea. So, I might have been happy about our accommodations, except that I didn't want to be there. Every little thing that bothered me prompted a, "I want to go back to Japan." It was the longest, saddest trip of my life.

People said that I looked like my older friend. She gave me her school uniform later, when uniforms were hard to find. Here, she is visiting from Kobe, after we moved to Hiroshima. Hiroshima, Jan 1943.

Wearing my friend's school uniform, when uniforms were hard to find after the war. The pin is my school pin. Osaka, May 1948.

First term, first year of high school, at my dream school. Only three or four of us have no uniform. Ichijo, in front of the school swimming pool, spring, 1946.

My first term, second year of high school. Students wore almost any uniform they could find even though uniforms were no longer required. Mine was from an older friend who attended a different school. The pin on my blouse is a school pin. The girl on the far right, second to top row, was my good friend and excellent artist. Osaka Fu Neyagawa Koto Jogako, May 1947.

First term, third year of high school. The teacher is our sewing teacher. Osaka Fu Neyagawa Koto Jogako, spring 1948.

Part way into my third year of high school after my high school became co-ed. The teacher is our music teacher. He took the girls to the NHK radio station before the boys joined our school. We sang on air and learned how sound effects were created in the studio. A giant basket of beans was used to make ocean sound effects from gentle lapping waves to crashing stormy seas. Osaka, Jul 1948.

Al, shortly after we met.

Our American wedding. Chapel of Hope,
Yokosuka Naval Base, 1956.

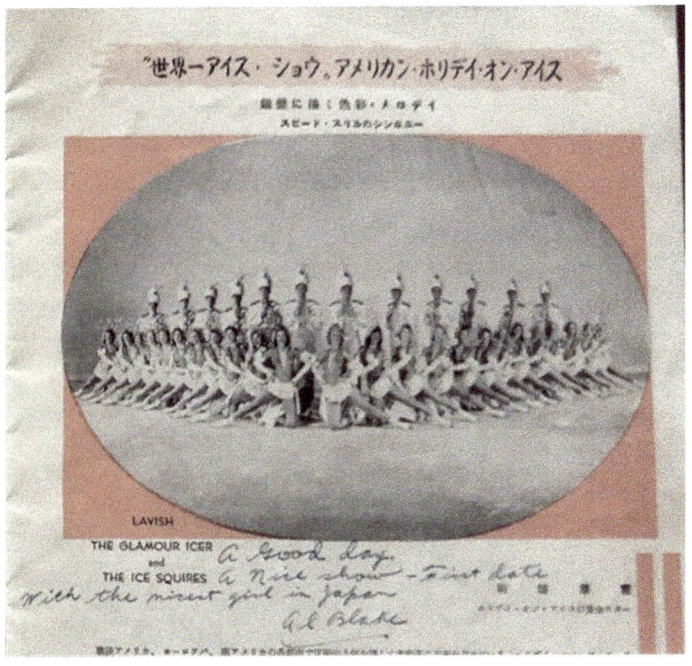

Holiday on Ice program from our first date. I didn't
know Al had kept this or made a note until I discovered
it 63 years later. The note reads "A good day. A nice
show – first date with the nicest girl in Japan"

Afterword

Interestingly, Kazuko's name, which was so troublesome for her in Japan because of its written form, was also problematic for her in her new country, but for a different reason. It is easily pronounced when looking at the letters when written in English, but the name itself is unusual in the U.S. It was so unusual that she immediately became "Kay" to everyone she met, starting with her father-in-law when she arrived at the port in Seattle. And soon after that, people began calling her "Chisai" when they heard Al using the moniker for "small" as a nickname for her.

Kazuko's father-in-law, Clarence Blake, greeted her and Al at the port in Seattle when they arrived from Japan. Clarence explained that Al's stepmother, a schoolteacher, was not able to be there because school was starting. She had driven with him to San Francisco, but when the ship was rerouted, she flew back to Iowa. Clarence, Al, and Kazuko traveled across the western states in Clarence's car, stopping in Salt Lake City where she met kind and friendly people, and Denver, where she learned her American shoe size, before an extended visit in Corning, Iowa. There she met her mother-in-law and other relatives. They made day trips to Des Moines to meet some of Al's friends, and then Clarence drove them to Minnesota to meet one of Al's sisters.

After a short visit, Clarence returned to Iowa, and Al and Kazuko took a train to Detroit, stopping briefly in Chicago. In Detroit, they took possession of a new car that Al had ordered from the Ford Motor Company. They continued their journey, stopping in Mansfield, Ohio, the Blue Ridge Mountain area, and Philadelphia, meeting more of Al's friends. The trip gave her a broad overview of the various cultures and lifestyles in the large country that was to be her new home.

When they arrived in Washington, D.C., she met more of his friends. Al was transferred to Patuxent River naval air base, where he was stationed for a couple years. His next assignment took them to Bainbridge, Maryland, for radio school, and then to

Norfolk and Virginia Beach, where he was stationed for seven years.

By the time Al retired from the U.S. Navy, Kazuko had developed close friendships with the wives of two of his coworkers. These Japanese women, Seiko and Kay quickly became honorary aunts to Kazuko's children. The three women and their families shared a lasting friendship despite subsequent moves separating them.

Even though she hadn't wanted to leave Japan, Kazuko faced the adventure of coming to a new country with strength and resilience. In the U.S. she encountered American features of those times: curious strangers, friendly and unfriendly faces, and some "Whites Only" signs in public places. Sometimes, she and Al had difficulty finding landlords who would accept them as renters because of her heritage, but others warmly welcomed her. Her adventures spanned the good and bad, too, but those are stories for another time.

Kazuko and Al raised three children together, settling in Richardson, Texas, after Al retired from the Navy. Kazuko reconnected with Sumi, her friend from

Itami Air Base and Yokosuka. She and her husband, Tom, had settled in Paris, Texas.

Al and Kazuko were active in their community and in their children's schooling and extracurricular activities. Both received numerous service awards and dedications from local schools, their church, and the city for their community service. After their children were grown and had left home, Kazuko reentered the work force, working until she was 80 years old, maintaining her own business for part of that time. Thirty years after Al passed away, Kazuko moved to southern Illinois, where she now resides with her son and near her oldest daughter. It was during that move that she discovered the old Holiday-on-Ice program with Al's handwritten note, "A good day. A nice show – First date with the nicest girl in Japan. . ."

Adapting to yet another new home, she continues to sew, garden, cook and bake for others, and bring joy to everyone around her.

My youngest daughter, Nola Lucke, and I at the A-Bomb
Dome in the Hiroshima Peace Memorial Park. I
accompanied her to Japan to watch her and her husband
run in the Tokyo Marathon. Hiroshima, March 2019.

Memorial to the Ichijo high school girls lost to the atomic bomb. It is located near the bridge from which many of the girls jumped into the river. Hiroshima, March 2019.

KAZUKO BLAKE is a retired professional seamstress and certified master of Ikebana, Japanese flower arranging. She is now in her 90s and lives with her son in O'Fallon, Illinois, where she continues to garden, cook, and sew. She keeps in touch with her friends and neighbors from Richardson, Texas, where she lived for 48 years.

SANDRA VEGA is one of Kazuko's daughters and a U.S. Air Force veteran. She is a graduate of the U. S. Air Force Academy and a grateful recipient of Kazuko's generosity and awesome parenting skills.

www.kazukostory.com

www.ingramcontent.com/pod-product-compliance
Lightning Source LLC
Chambersburg PA
CBHW051313120626
46547CB00015B/2220